INKVERSE

Tits and Bits of Life

Samta Ranka

BookLeaf Publishing

India | USA | UK

Dedication

To the silent moments,
the whispered dreams,
and the untold stories that live in every heart.

To those who feel deeply, love fiercely,
and find solace in the rhythm of words—
this collection is for you.

And to the one within me,
who never stopped writing,
even when the world went quiet.

So, this is something from my heart to yours!!!

Preface

Poetry has always been my way of observing, feeling, and understanding the world. This collection is a reflection of moments — both delicate and intense — captured in verse.

The poems in this book stem from personal experiences, quiet musings, and everyday wonders. They speak of love, loss, hope, nature, and the inner conversations we often do silence.

Through this book, I hope to connect with readers who find comfort in rhythm, healing in words, and meaning in metaphors. This is not just a collection of poems — it is a piece of my heart shared with you.

I started writing poems when I was 11.Here, I am now writing this book and fulfilling my checklist of dreams.

Thank you for being a part of this journey.

Acknowledgements

I would like to express my heartfelt gratitude to all those who have supported me throughout the journey of this poetry collection.

First and foremost, my deepest thanks to my parents, family for their unwavering love, encouragement, and belief in my words. To my friends who read my poems every time, offered feedback, and shared their own emotions and book leaf publishing for taking my poems to the world. Thank you for being part of this creative voyage.

A special mention to my mentors and teachers who inspired me to explore the world of poetry and helped me find my voice.

Finally, I am grateful to every reader who holds this book in their hands — may these poems speak to your soul as they did to mine.

1. A message to oneself.

There is a heart inside **bones and flesh**,
To which I am here to address.
You are secure and safer,
My worthy amateur.
Often you are not practical,
Without you I am not able.
You break ,you heal,
You move on with zeal,
I know many stitches you have both old and new,
I will try harder to keep you happy, as **I m no one
without you**.

2. A Call to Happiness

Oh happiness !abide me,
Thou surround with glee,
Fill life with thy drops of ecstasy,
Saturated without jealousy.

Oh joy ! come on we will enjoy,
To have thy jocund company,
Having forgotten all purgatories,
Filling life with thy remedies.

Oh thou laughter!
Pick me up from gutter,
Help me to flee,
Towards cheerful glee.

Oh smile! come on my lips,
Teach thy overwhelming tips,
Prevent me from nostalgia,
And never bid me, See Ya

3. The Breeze of Comfort

I was drenched in thoughts ,
But, you flew across like a breeze,
Vaporizing the whistling rots,
And hugging me with a gentle ease.
So deeply soaked was I,
But, the coolest in you made me dry,
You noticed something too light ,too translucent in the eyes.
You noticed the heaviness , the smile that lies.

4. The Fragile Balance of Confidence

Yes,she is lost,
May be it happens with the most,
But its something unusual,
Seemingly non-perennial.

Beauty was noticed but surpassed,
Her outlook stands biased,
Lacunas are concentrated more,
May be for getting something galore.

A perfect human tendency,
Where pessimism is the first fancy,
Optimism is just a dim ray,
Struggling to find its way.

Deficits need attention,
Losing confidence is not the intention,
Improving is the necessity,
Because deficits arise dubeity.

With time all of it fades,
Things will move on!!Comrade,

Today is tougher, tomorrow will be tough,
So the difficulties diminished enough.

5. Memories

If past could become present,
Why only memories they sent?
If then could become now,
Because memories are just wow,
Can you provide me a time machine?
To relive the happiest life's scene.
BECAUSE
Memories we make together,
Stories they become later,
A little source of laughter,
Is relieving to remember.

6. The Sun and Its Flower

If I am the sunflower,
You have been the sun,
You have been the light,
Facing which things go right.
In my world , you are at a great place,
I am so tiny, I need your light to ace.

I m not enough, I know,
But I don't need the snow,
I need the sun,
And be the silly one,
Loved ,cared, angered, teased,
In your warmth ,blanketed.

I wish to do everything and many things that I don't
with you,
Please let me be your favorite sunflower, make no new,
Wishing is not enough ,nor am I,
So ,would u stop bidding HI.???
Is this too much to ask for,
Am I expecting things galore.

I bloom because of you,
I will droop without you,

And am being too much sensitive right,
Like the touch me not plant, me being leave me not
flower.
Dear sun, you rarely change like the phases of the moon,
And the sensitivity in me wishes the all time noon .

7. Threads of Duty

Happiness hugged the heart of the sister,
When she heard about arrival of her brother,
Raksha bandhan was the soul event of the time,
But agony occupied the air with phone's chime.
His words were,
"Border awaits me and I need to be there
Protection of nation is as important as rakhi I wear."
Now say-
'What do you want as return gift?
That will just stand at courier's rift.'
Sister replied,
'I need no gift from you by courier,
I need your presence on rakhi next year.'
For the next few days war was on,
Awaiting her brother ,she sat forlorn.
Somebody arrived and said-
"Your brother is no more,
I salute him from my heart's core."
She read out his note,
That he lastly wrote,
'My presence for next rakhi won't be as satisfactory,
As-our country India's unforgettable victory.'

8. A Bond Beyond Waters

Old man questioned little girl Mony,
Why are you sitting lonely?
Where is your mother?
Girl in reply went out of shelter.
Pointed out to sky high,
Where her mother lie.

Victims of flood were they,
When on a rock they lay.
With house filled with water,
With no straw's roof over.
Had one sweater to wear,
Which mother gave to daughter.
In cold weather and rain,
As they suffered from pain.

When they were waiting for rescuers,
Her mother got high fever.
She went in search of stars,
From her very far.
Rescued Mony awaited her mother's return,
In the hot, bright and scorching sun.

Old man understood the situation,

He took Mony to his mansion.
They were victims of a flood,
In which men lost their blood.
In which two souls were made apart,
But they were always in each other's heart.

9. The Art of Letting Go

The art of letting go
Is a kind of picturesque grace,
A skill we must embrace.

Scrolling taught this subtle art,
So vital, so beautiful.
Because, my dear reader,
You deserve so many things.
Your heart is a mirror,
Not meant to shatter like broken wings.

Instead, let it reflect the light within,
You are a gem, aren't you?
Value yourself, shine brighter.
Let the gloom lift,
Perhaps by letting go.

For those you love and truly care for,
For the ones who are meant to stay,
Holding on too tightly
Only weighs you down.
And in this heaviness, you drain,
Your eyes releasing too much pain.

Don't you think it's time?
Keep your little heart light,
Move forward with a smile.
Because-
Days walk,
Minutes jog,
And seconds run.

Live your life, my dear reader,
For happiness comes from within.
Just learn the art of letting go.
Erase the hollows, the excess,
All the blacks and whites—
And notice the **VIBGYOR** in the sky.

Let the colors fill your face, too.

10. Tiding thoughts

My thoughts are never steady ,
To roam around they are always ready ,
From voyage of books it elicits me,
Murmuring doctor, scientist, or dentist, to be.

Dilemma becomes an unwanted friend,
Making me my own mind's fiend ,
It sways along rivers, changing tributaries ,
Taking me towards war of wearies.

Thoughts are like never-ending ladder,
Grinding me along with the batter,
 Where beginning and ending is similar,
 But reason for apprehension is unfamiliar.

I find myself in a garden of rose ,
During mares when I dose,
Bewildering me if I am silly,
Or my thoughts are willy.

Hallucinations never leave me away,
Rather like periodic tides, always stay ,
Washing away the precious time ,instead of the sand,
Proving my incapacity to control mind's magic wand.

11. The Quiet Call

That soundless soliloquy echoes,
Amidst the screwing chaos ,
Somewhere near the kernel ,it had originated,
Then ,to the brain it was communicated,
There it was read as a message,
Where truth was under a leakage ,
When the outer self sounds false,
The inner self gives true calls.

12. Mirage of the Mind

In the world of illusions,
We live in hallucinations,
Apparently,somewhere sea and sky meets,
But are we answered ,where each quits?
Apparently, sky is touched by mountain tops,
Although somewhere before it stops,
Apparently sky is the bed of stars and moon,
And also of the sun in the noon.
What one sees might be an illusion,
So think before jumping into any conclusion.

13. Wings of Spirit

Try to be the wings,
With the rhythm of air that swings,
Confront the currents of breeze and gust,
Fly forward on its abilities' trust,
So with confidence face challenges,
And be the definition of spirits' visage.

14. Golden Skies, Heavy Feet

While purgatories are pricking,
Why ecstasy keeps knocking?
It's hard opening your gateway,
In which pain costs the pay.

You dream of skies with golden hue,
Yet walk through storms that darken you.
Each step a whisper, a stinging plea,
A toll you pay to set joy free.

The shadows cling like second skin,
And silence echoes deep within.
But still, a rhythm soft and low,
Keeps knocking where your sorrows grow.

For buried deep beneath the ache,
Are seeds of dawn that long to wake.
Ecstasy waits not at ease,
But dances with your tragedies.

So let the purging fire burn,
Let every twist and trial churn—

For through the gates where pain once stayed,
a brighter soul may be remade.

15. A Maze Called Me

I am lost somewhere between aim and dream,
Where ambitions whisper, but visions scream.
Between what I plan and what I feel,
In a tug of war between fake and real.

I am lost somewhere between solitary and seen,
In quiet corners, where I've always been.
Craving the crowd, yet loving the hush,
Longing for voices, yet drawn to the hush.

I am lost somewhere between promise and trust,
In words once golden, now fading to dust.
Between hands held tight and hearts set free,
Between "stay with me" and "let me be."

I am lost somewhere between mind and heart,
Logic says leave, emotions won't part.
Torn by the silence between each beat,
Where thoughts retreat and feelings meet.

I am lost between sunrise and setting sun,
Between what's ended and just begun.
I walk a path that no one sees,
Carving answers into fallen leaves.

I am lost but maybe I'm meant to be,
For in this maze, I'm finding me.
In every tear and every smile,
I'm learning to stay lost for a while.

16. Aimless Echoes

What are you worth for?
Questions my heart's core.
My mind does freeze.,
My heart grunts like bees,
My heart goes lub-dub, lub-dub,
To which my actions do dub.
Should I walk left to right or straight?
Or for life should I wait?
I am unable to hear knocks at the door,
I feel lost like a boat without an oar,
I'm totally confused.
My inner light has fused.
Am I ambitionless?
Do I walk missionless?
I do not know what do I need to do,
As what's my aim, I'm unable to pursue

17. Love is in the air

Love is like a beautiful ,red flower,
For some sweet fragrance does it shower,
Hence they say, love is in the air,
Keep it away from evil eyes' pair.
For some it is spine on stems,
With some unfulfilled dreams.
Pricking directly to the center of the heart,
Alike arrow penetrating the center of the dart,
For some envelope of red petals,
Having higher value than opals,
As beautiful as to give,
As beautiful as to receive.

18. Stair Towards the Twinkling Star

A stair toward a twinkling star,
Is what I've been chasing from afar.
Too often, I'm miffed at my worn-out shoes,
That slip me into trials I didn't choose.
Each step unfolds a brand-new test,
Conquered only by giving my best.
Still, I climb, no matter how far,
For success is hard work's final star.

19. Dawn's Victory

Sunshine crawled in,
Gloominess it did win,
It bleached the chamber,
By the rays sun utter.

20. Rising Through Pages

She walked through shadow's slim,
With her voice a whisper-frail and dim.
A vermilion streak marked her fate,
Abide by the rules ,she did never create.

Flickering amidst the howling gust,
She tried to stand still and just,
She managed to ignite the light within,
The fire of gaining knowledge kept her keen.

With books in hand she proved,
'Pen is mightier than sword',
When world asked her, **'STAY WITHIN'**,
She turned pages and prepared to win.

Kamala Harris-a lady bold and strong,
Showed who belongs to the throng,
Kiran Bedi who has been perfect in her work,
Has already etched her name as a permanent mark.

Kalpana Chawla and Sunita Willams showed what
happens when women fly,
They unfolded their wings to touch the limitless sky,
Marie Curie with her idea in Science,

Brought about radiance's renaissance.

They are all just bits of crowds scattered,
The ones who battled and achieved,
What if every women achieve education?
They can turn the tables of whole nation.

'Beti Bachao Beti Padhaao' peaks,
The orthodox society breaks,
If some with hurdles can achieve so much,
Then all with facilities can achieve a bunch.

Lets not entangle their threads,
Lets free them making sky their beds,
Lets let them hover high like a kite,
Lets us see their episode of tomorrow's light.

21. The aura of Examination

It starts with searching of seats,
With increasing heart beats,
Not for the fear of examination,
But for the fear of anticipation,
About,if good friends will surround,
Or answer sheets will be ready for red round.

What follows next is complete trauma,
With gliding thoughts of fullstop and comma,
Complete bewilderment starts in mind,
When hellish questions we find,
Eyes glide to nearby table,
Complled to shatter exam's preamble.

When unknown questions arise,
There are expectations in the eyes,
To the one who is sitting anigh,
Skipping the thought , "SHOULD I?"
Answers are copied from paper to paper,
Under the eyes of surveilling teachers.

Whispers are heard from front,back,left and right,
Attentiveness to each sound heard and signal's sight,
Is the complete aura of examination hall,

The place that denotes student's rise and fall,
Happiness is the end of examinations,
Resulting in fleeting of all apprehensions.

22. We will meet again

From a little distance,
With some coincidence,
On a street,
We will meet,
We will meet again.

By quiet coincidence,
At a crowded street,
Our paths will cross,
And once again,
We will meet.
We will meet again.

Amid the city's constant race,
Putting aside the frantic pace,
We'll pause and share a smile,
Talk and linger for a while,
We will meet.
We will meet again

By some happenstance,
At an instance,
On a street,

We will meet,
We will meet again.

23. School's Butterfly Days

In school unknown faces met,
Years ago together we sat,
A bond of friendship grew in between,
This is how started all school's scenes.

Many years did pass,
Passing our 10 th class,
But memories flush in mind,
When to oneself lonely will find.

Throwing chalks on one another,
Getting scoldings from the teacher,
Going to washroom with our gang,
Continuing gossip till bell rang.

Sharing a single chocolate among eight,
Not submitting copies before respective date,
Teasing others in the name of other,
Like putting honey over butter.

In every annual function there were no studies,
When we enjoyed with our fellow buddies,
By taking cell phones to school,
Is how we broke the rule.

Gossiping during speeches,
As well as in boring classes,
Was our common habit,
Though we didn't get any credit.

During exams being dependent on each other,
For some of the answers of the chapter,
Using our own language of communication,
With front or back benchers concatenation.

Playing pen fighting by being back benchers,
Or hand cricket by constituting team members,
Making a group for truth and dare,
When eyeballs on bottle stare.

Roaming in corridor with friends,
In the name of notes taken in hands,
A school's day ends with a last bell,
To me which seemed like an angel.

Joking with teachers,
Naming them further,
Sometimes among friends getting angry,
Next moment rejoicing was our journey.

We have had our farewell,

We have heard that last day's last school bell,
Promising to remain in contact with one another,
Least realizing ,**'OUR BUTTERFLY DAYS WERE OVER'.**

24. Undervalued Therapy

When tears kiss my cheek,
It's not that I m weak,
But pain is on its peak,
For remedy to be quick.

It washes down my pain,
Prevents me from being insane,
It gives me some tablets of relief,
To end up with an optimistic belief.

25. A Letter to 10 years old Samta

Dear 10 years old Samta,
This is a letter from 20 years old Samta.

In this journey from you to me,
A lot of differences I do see,
You are a thin, little, frail cute girl,
Whose hair just touched shoulders with a curl,
Now this is me, tall ,probably fat , working and studying adult,
Whose hair often manages to touch her denim's belt.

Though physically we are different, we are one,
Because in the veins same blood run.
With similar faces we give different look,
Because what differs is the cover of book.

Whenever I act cringe, you reflect in mind,
With essence of euphoria and values you bind,
A soul of innocence comes to me,
With qualities evaporated from my cup of tea.

You continue to exist in me,
In my memories you survive,

Sooner ,I will be older than you by 10 years plus 1,
Because watering of each year never allows the burn.

Dear 10 years old Samta,
You are me ,I am you,
No one is old ,no one is new,
Let moments sew,
Till then ADIEU!